BIBLIOTHERAPY

Bibliotherapy

A COLLECTION OF POETRY

By

Frannie Gilbertson

ADELAIDE BOOKS

New York / Lisbon

2024

BIBLIOTHERAPY
A collection of poetry
By Frannie Gilbertson

Published by Adelaide Books, New York / Lisbon

adelaidebooks.org

Editor-in-Chief: Stevan V. Nikolic

For any information, please address Adelaide Books LLC
at editor@adelaidebooks.org

ISBN: 978-1-958419-96-0

Printed in the United States of America

For my parents.

Without you I wouldn't know how to read or write.

I have you to thank for this gift.

Contents

Part One: The Reader

Part Two: The Author

Part One
THE READER

Need

Like an engine needs oil

Like a pen needs ink

Like a body needs blood

Life needs literature.

Literature

What is a book but the wings

by which a person can sail

a ship of curiosity

into a sea of possibility.

The Library

Take me

to a place

where the poetry flows

like a river

and the novels greet you

like old friends.

Bookstores

Bookstores are unique places.

They have shelves full of creatures from uncharted lands,

Heroes and heroines fighting demons and monsters to save their families,

Ordinary boys and girls, boys and boys, girls and girls falling in love between the pages of an unexpected romance that only a select few will be able to share with them.

They are places to hide and places to shine,

places to dream and places to act,

places to fear and places to embrace.

It is all here amongst the rows and rows of ancient parchment that trees gave their last breaths to become.

A second life,

a reincarnation of sorts, books are,

but bookstores…

Bookstores are where the dreamers go.

They are where the lovers embrace

and the adventurers roam.

They are where the poets sleep

and the lonely hearts meet.

They are where the broken hearts go to recover

and the bitter souls go to mourn.

Bookstores are doors to the people we seek to be, the people we are, and the people we once were too afraid to face.

Where Hemingway and Poe can mingle and share drunken pasts that only they can understand.

Bookstores are where Ray Bradbury, Kurt Vonnegut, and Harper Lee can toast to the stories that others were too closed-minded to read.

They are where the Bronte sisters and Jane Austen can laugh and flirt with the lovers they never aim to please.

Bookstores are where Emily Dickinson and Emily Barret Browning can weep for their sorrows and dance in their triumphs.

Bookstores are where artists go to write and be written about.

They are peace and comfort,

anger and sorrow,

love and sensuality,

They are a place of wonder.

Bookstores are magic.

And I, within them, become magic too.

Adventure

I want to get lost.
Lost in a place that only exists in my imagination
lost in the lives of people I will never meet
lost in a fantasy of my own making.

I want to be so lost that I forget my name and
decide to take the last one of my fictional love instead.
I want to forget my life and forge a new one
between the pages of a novel only I understand.

I want to get lost
and never be found.

Between the Pages

"Between the pages of books is a wonderful place to be," they said.

But they didn't tell me about the years' worth of emotional damage

you'd find within those pages.

You find your favorite character only for them to let you down two chapters later.

You fall in love with the most beautiful man or woman in the existence of literature

but then you learn they are spoken for someone else.

You begin to enjoy hanging out with the side character that you thought you'd surely hate,

however the author decides they need to go sit in literary heaven in the sequel.

Between the pages of a book will have you asking yourself "where is my letter?"

and "do I choose to run with the fearless outcasts or give up myself for a life of selfless service?"

You will no longer think of an unsharpened pencil as a premature writing utensil but instead as a magical instrument that chose you.

You will find yourself thinking in every jewelry store you enter

that there is a ring destined to take you on an adventure you
have no idea if you'll return from.

Between the pages of a book you will see the worst in people

and sometimes realize that the very same monster lives inside of
you, too.

You will see your favorite character violated and desecrated.

You will see them break.

You will see them lose their battles with their enemies, their
friends,

and themselves.

You will see them in *you*

and it will terrify you.

terrify you so much that you must leave their world for a bit and
return to your own.

You will attach yourself to people you will never know.

You will fall in love in the most unlikely of places.

You will travel more than anyone in the world.

All because you found yourself in between the pages of a book.

With Gratitude

To the young adult section of the bookstore:
Thank you for being my place of comfort
when I couldn't find it for myself.

Comfort Read

If I could
I'd wrap myself up in my favorite stories.

Like a quilt of comfort and fantasy,
books for me are a security blanket for
which my soul desperately clings to.

Dear Book Characters

I wish you were real.

I wish I could hold your hand

or wrap my arms around you in the tightest hug I've ever given.

I wish I could laugh with you,

ask you questions,

cry,

tell you how many heartbreaks and insecurities you have saved me from.

I wish I could tell you about the inspiration you bring me.

Because of you, I can give life to my own paper people.

I can make something beautiful and impactful out of keys and ink.

I desperately wish you were real.

I wish for it so deeply that it leaves me gasping for breath and begging for you to be made of flesh and life rather than words and imagination.

But alas, the gods will not let me have you.

Instead you will exist in the corner of my mind

where you will be immortal,

happy.

A place where you'll be safe:

safe from fear,

safe from pain,

safe from everything.

A place where when I wander between the spaces of paper, I am left with what I already know:

I wish so much that you were real.

Beauty

I will never see your face
I will never hear your voice
I will never know your touch
or the scent of your hair.

I will never know the kindness in your eyes
or the taste of your lips
I will never sleep in your arms
or wake up to your smile

So instead I will settle for your words
and I will love you so deep that the
library shelves will sing of our affair
long after the last word is written

The Beast

so push me against the shelves

wrap your hands around my mind

and whisper ideas into my imagination

So that I may write you into the

library log of my heart.

Book Boyfriend

You were real
I held your hand through your confessions
I cried when you were in pain
I heard your laughter from a world away.

You were real.

I hunted down your enemies
I rejoiced in your triumphs
I screamed during your death
You were real.

I know because
when I was falling apart it was your
embrace that I sought.
When I heard my favorite songs it was you
I wanted to dance with.
When I was lonely it was your
words I wept for.

You are real.

V/L/R/S

And so, darling,
I will sing lullabies to the stars
and rejoice at the moon
for it is there between the pages
wrapped in sheets of darkness
that I find you

and my soul will forever weep
for your laughter until I hear it again.

Resolution

What is a library but a field of wildflowers
for a reader to pick into a bouquet of wisdom.

We will put them in vases to display on
a shelf of antiquities

to be wielded like antidotes for a plague of ignorance
or weapons for a war on speech.

We will sharpen our words and trim our pages
to hang into banners of triumph
over our paper castles that we built with thoughts
of publishing what antagonists wanted so badly to silence.

The Banned

We are the vessels

for a revolution

of the next generation

that will bathe in the blood

of those that threaten

our liberation.

A Burning Book

You can break my spine,

rip out my pages,

and burn my words

but just like the witches by whose hands

I was created

I will survive.

Bibliophile

I am a bibliophile

I don't just read the book
I dive into the book.

I smuggle myself between the pages and
write myself into the chapters

I inhale the printed words
and absorb them into my skin.

I am a bibliophile.

I don't just read the book
I become the book.

Acknowledgements

Because of a book,
I have a writer's soul
and a reader's imagination.

Plot Twist

Then there comes a day
when the reader
becomes the author;

for her mind is too full
to be left unread.

Part Two
THE AUTHOR

Friends To Lovers

You were written into my life with no explanation

but then your words became a romance novel
and your smile became poetry

and suddenly
we became a trope.

SMUT

And so I will open you like a book,

slipping my fingers between the pages of your body

and reading the words of your soul.

Read Me

Read me like your favorite book:

Caress the cover of my life

Flip through the pages of my heart

Bookmark your favorite memories

and display me on the shelf with your favorite novels.

Book Binding

You told me you were a used book
with torn binding and fading ink

So I took my pen
and wrote beauty back
into your decaying pages and
reglued your broken pieces

So we could live in my library
forever.

Revision

Let me annotate the curves of your body with my tongue
and erase the insecurities of your mind with my fingers.

The Pen

I will write you in sonnets

and stack them into towers so high

Belle's library will envy my collection

The Sword

but then you ripped up my drafts
and set fire to our story

Now the archives hold no record of us.

Papercut

They say heartbreak is like death by a thousand cuts
but whoever said that must have never felt the sting of
a writer's wrath.

Bleed

I was too immersed in our fiction that I couldn't see the pages were giving me papercuts.

FMC

You made my words flow like ink from a pen

But you scrambled my thoughts like words in a draft.

Alternate Ending

I should've ended it when you told me
you'd never feel the same, but I couldn't
stop writing poems about you

and I don't know how to change that.

Immortality

Even if my words dry up

and my inkwell becomes empty

I will still rip myself open and

bleed my heart dry until our story

is recorded.

Epic

I knew I needed to purge you from my story
so I cut myself open and bled my pain onto the page

but no matter how many times I write
you out of me, you'll remain.

You are the epic I will never be rid of.

Cliffhanger

You wrote your words onto my skin in permanent ink
and never even finished the book

Now I'm stuck in the labyrinth
of rereading a story with no resolution.

Fiction

I prefer fantasy to reality because that is
where I can find you still wrapped in the
ink of our own novel that never received
the ending it deserved.

Checked Out

I saw our happy ending in your eyes
But all you saw was the return date in mine.

To Be Read

I'll never tell you but I wish you were still mine.

I'll never tell you but I wonder if your lips would still be soft against my own.

I'll never tell you but I wish I could run my fingers through your hair,

slipping through the strands like a knife through melted butter.

I'll never tell you but I think of you often

late at night when no one can hear and the secrets between us can run wild

like the wind through my window.

I'll never tell you but I wished I would've listened.

I'll never tell you

And so these musings will sit of the To Be Read shelf of my mind

gathering dust until I find the courage to pick them up again.

Bonus Chapter

And so we slip into our secret garden
full of roses and trees
where I can kiss you beneath the stars in
the shadowed safety of our private affair

but roses have thorns
and trees can rot

so why am I surprised that you closed
our book on an ellipsis?

Editing Process

I spent so long

trying to force a plot

that wouldn't work

that I neglected to think

of the joy that could come

from editing you out of

my life.

Annotation

And just like that

the page turned and you were nothing
but a footnote in the margin of my past.

The End

I used to be afraid of the unexpected
fearful of closing the book

But when I did

My fingers itched with an excitement
that only a blank page could offer.

Frannie Gilbertson

Author's Note

The first people I need to acknowledge are my family. None of my writing would exist without them, so this is their published poetry collection too.

Mom, thank you for teaching me how to read and staying on me about school and my education. My love of reading started with you since you read those first words to me. You always encouraged me to have a book in my hand and now I never leave the house without one.

Dad, thank you for paying for a private education. The opportunities I was given because of you led me to even be able to send this collection off in the first place. I will always be appreciative of everything you've done for me and being my biggest fan along the way.

Grand, thank you for always encouraging my love of writing just as much as you encouraged my reading. You have always believed I could do this and there were a few times I doubted I'd succeed. I should know better than to argue with you when your mind is set.

To my best friends, you are the only three people that probably understand just how much this collection means to me because it's about one of my favorite things in the world. You three have always understood my love of reading and have held my hand through so many bookish journeys. And now I've corrupted you to read all the dirty novels with me mwahahaha!

To my 600 peeps, y'all are the best accountabili-buddies a girl could ask for! I'm so thankful to have you each in my life and I can't wait to give you each a copy of this when it comes out!

Frannie Gilbertson

To my lover, thank you for putting up with my mood swings and all-day lock-ins. Thank you for being a proofreader of this collection and one of my biggest supporters. I love you to the moon and back, honeybee.

About the Author

Frannie Gilbertson is a shortlist winner nominee of the 2024 Adelaide Literary Award Contest in the category of Poetry, with her work titled Bookstores.

Frannie Gilbertson is a native of Fort Worth, TX and has an English degree from Texas Wesleyan University. She completed her first full novel in middle school and has been writing ever since. She published her first novel, *The Secret of Us* as a senior in high school and is now the self-published author of the *Fast Lane* series on Amazon Direct Publishing. Frannie writes in all genres most notably fiction and poetry and is frequently featured in *Adelaide Literary Magazine*. She is also an avid reader of all things dark romance and fantasy and is a major Swiftie! When not reading or writing, you can find her taking pictures for her bookstagram (@littlelovelyreads).